BIBLE PATTERNS FC

TWO WEEKS WITH PAUL

A Shipwreck

Lee Jenkins   **Illustrated by Todd Jenkins**

ISBN (paperback): 978-1-956457-08-7
ISBN (ebook): 978-1-956457-09-4

Book design: Christy Collins, Constellation Book Services
E-book design: Maggie McLaughlin
Publishing consultant: Martha Bullen, Bullen Publishing Services

Printed in the United States of America

Look for current and future titles by Lee Jenkins within these series:

Bible Patterns for Young Readers
>A Day with Jesus: The Story of Zacchaeus
>A Week with Joshua: The Battle of Jericho
>An Evening With Daniel: The Lions' Den Theatre
>Five Years Protecting Jesus: A Christmas Story
>A Very Long Day with Elijah: The Contest
>An Exciting Night with Peter: A Jailbreak
>Three Days with Jonah: A Whale of a Story
>Eight Days with Thomas: An Easter Story
>A Year with Naomi: From Sad to Glad
>Three Days of Prayer: Esther's Miracle

Aesop Patterns for Young Readers
>The Thirsty Crow: Aesop's Little by Little Fable
>Who's Afraid of a Lion? Aesop's Bully Fable
>Yummy, Yummy, Yummy, Honey, Honey, Honey:
>>Aesop's Groupthink Fable
>Sour Grapes: Aesop's Fooling Yourself Fable

Pattern Block Stories for Young Readers

Other books by Lee Jenkins:
>How to Create a Perfect School
>Optimize Your School
>From Systems Thinking to Systemic Action
>Permission to Forget: And Nine Other Root
>>Causes of America's Frustration with Education

Two Weeks with Paul: A Shipwreck
Background Knowledge

Paul wrote to the church in Rome, "I long to see you...I planned many times to come to you." In the same letter Paul also wrote, "We know that for those who love God, all things work together for good for those also called according to his purpose."

Paul delivered gifts from churches in Asia and Europe to Christians in Jerusalem. While there, evil people attempted to kill Paul for preaching about Jesus. He was taken to Caesarea for his safety, but kept in prison while Felix, a Roman official, hoped Paul would pay a bribe for his release.

After two years, Paul was shipped to Rome to be judged by Caesar. Although Paul had every reason to be afraid, he chose to continue worshiping God and preaching about Jesus. God used this time to accomplish amazing things such as:

- While in prison, Paul taught three Roman officials (Felix, Festus, and Agrippa) about the power and love of Jesus. His message to Agrippa has been read by billions of people.
- 274 people from different countries learned about the power and love of Jesus while in a terrible storm and shipwreck.
- The ship attempted to sail 40 miles from one Crete harbor to a better harbor on Crete and was blown off course for two weeks to the island of Malta. The people of Malta experienced Jesus' love through healing and Paul's teaching for three months during the winter.
- Paul's travel companion Luke waited near Caesarea and Jerusalem for two years because Paul could have been released any day. We do not know when Luke interviewed Mary and gave the world most of the knowledge we have about the birth of Jesus. It is likely that Luke interviewed Mary while waiting for Paul's release from prison.

All things did work together for good!
Acts 21-28; Romans 1:11, 1:13 and 8:28

Paul and Luke joined 274 sailors and passengers.

The wind blew softly.

The waves were calm.

The sailors and
passengers relaxed.

The sailors and passengers watched the sea.

The winds began to howl.

The winds made
the ship go left.

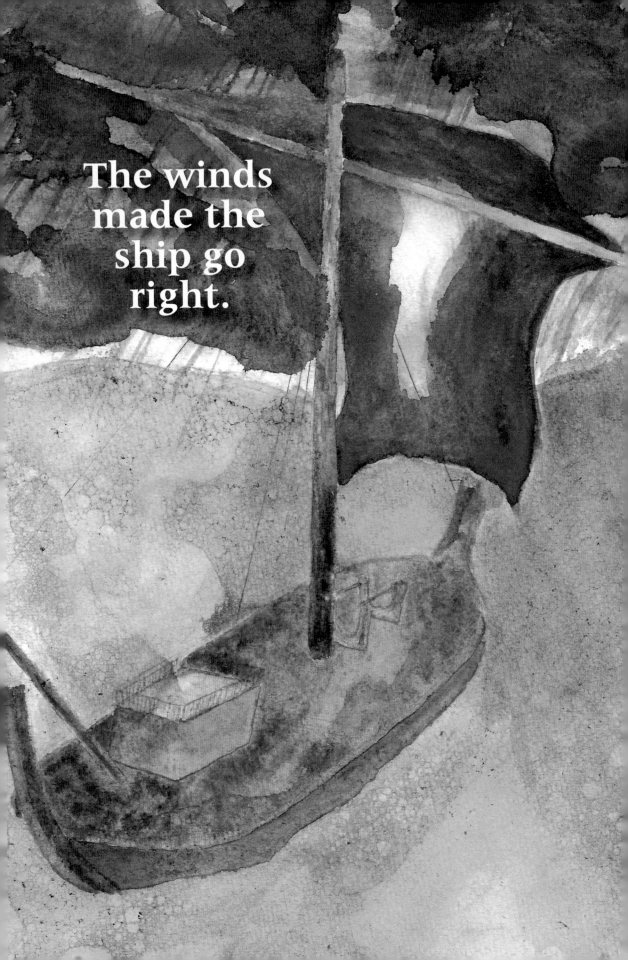

The winds
made the
ship go
right.

The waves
made the
ship go up.

**The waves made
the ship go down.**

Sailors and passengers
watched the sea
even more.

The winds howled
and yowled.

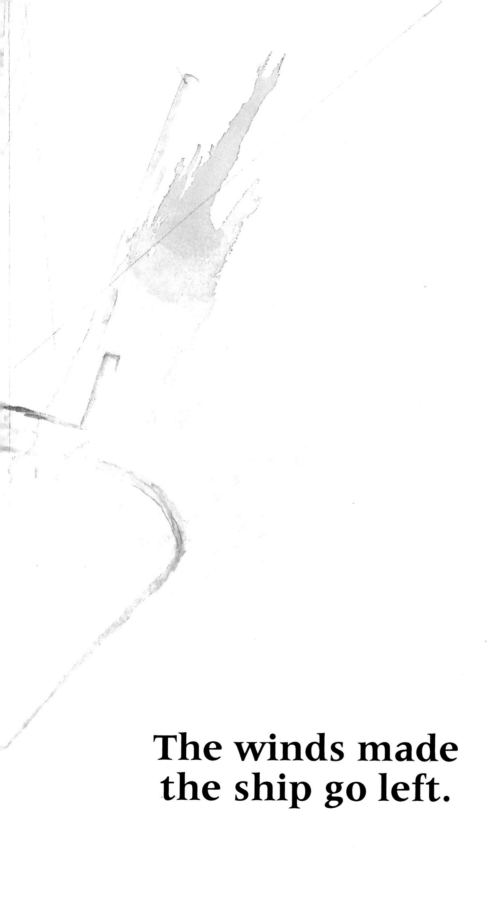

**The winds made
the ship go left.**

The winds made the
ship go right.

The waves made the
ship go up and up.

The waves made
the ship
go down

and down.

Really, really
scared

sailors
and
passengers
watched
the sea
a lot
more.

**The winds howled,
yowled and growled.**

**The winds made
the ship go left.**

**The winds made
the ship go right.**

The waves
made the
ship go up,
up and up.

The waves made the
ship go down, down,
and down.

An angel told Paul
nobody would drown.

The sailors and passengers were really, really, really scared.

Paul told Luke what the angel told him.

Paul told the sailors
and passengers

that God would keep
them all safe.

The ship crashed
on a sandbar.

The sailors,
passengers,
Paul and Luke

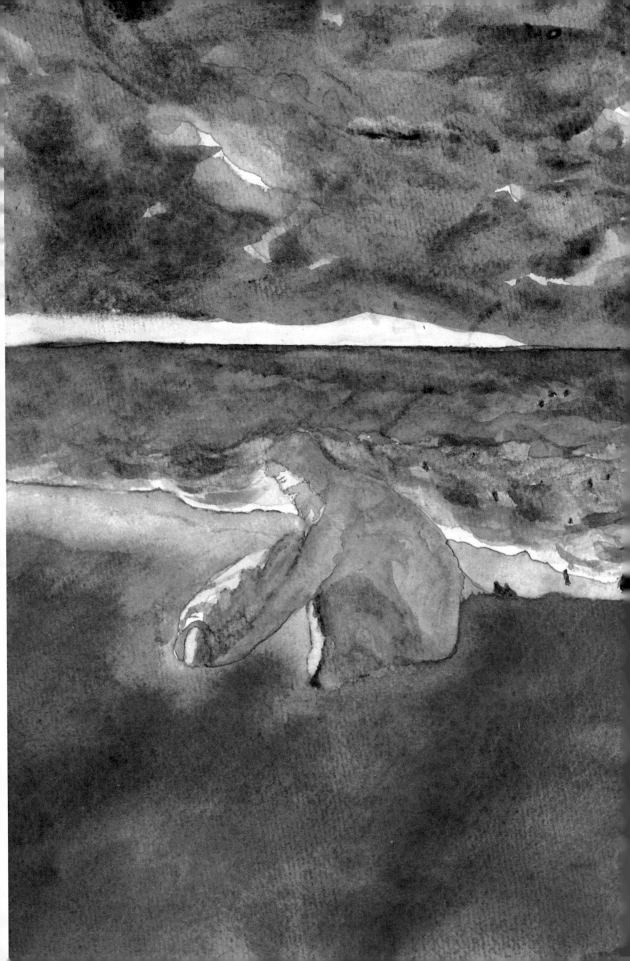

swam safely to

the island of Malta.

Parents and Young Readers

Children intuitively believe they can learn to read. The best way parents can support their children in their reading journey is by maintaining this inborn belief and confidence, especially during their early reading years (between ages 4-8). One way parents can do this is by providing reading materials that include predictable patterns. Many early reading books use patterns, such as rhyming words, alliteration, counting, or the alphabet. Our brains search for patterns because patterns make sense.

When children recognize a pattern and complete it for themselves, their confidence soars. Increased confidence fuels a child's drive to read and lays the foundation for future reading.

The Bible Patterns for Young Readers series is written with as many patterns as possible for each Bible story. The complete Bible story usually cannot be told with patterns alone, however. That's why these books are designed as a parent/child reading experience. First, the parent reads the complete book several times out loud to the child. The child soon identifies and reads the patterned parts of the book, while the parent reads details that are not patterned. This partnership is beautiful to witness.

There are times in a child's life to slow down and sound out a word, but too many of these "slowdowns" create an obstacle and distaste for reading. What children need to maintain their confidence is to hear themselves read a book at the same pace and with the same voice inflections and pauses as an adult. Eventually, children will read the whole story on their own. They will proudly read it to family, friends, and grandparents.

Let us keep the joy of reading alive! Learning to read should be so painless that children forget how they learned to read, but the stories so powerful they are remembered for life.

We can do this: parents and children together can share a love of reading.

Made in the USA
Columbia, SC
29 March 2022

58274671R00022